Starr King
in
California

by

William Day Simonds

Starr King in California
by William Day Simonds

ISBN: 978-93-67144-42-8

Published by

DOUBLE 9 BOOKS

2/13-B, Ansari Road
Daryaganj, New Delhi – 110002
info@double9books.com
www.double9books.com
Tel. 011-40042856

ABOUT THE AUTHOR

William Day Simonds uses words to craft experiences, convey ideas, and capture imaginations. He operates at the intersection of creativity and communication, sculpting narratives that range from vivid fiction to enlightening non-fiction. His process involves not just writing, but also research, observation, and a profound understanding of human emotions and societal dynamics. His works reflect a wide array of influences, from personal experiences to historical events. His narratives can transport readers to fantastical worlds, explore complex psychological landscapes, and present new viewpoints on familiar topics. The diversity in his approach—from the tone and structure of their prose to the themes he explores—ensures that his work resonates with different audiences in unique ways. His contributions to literature and discourse have shaped cultural trends, challenge conventions, and inspire others. By presenting ideas in innovative ways, he plays a crucial role in expanding the boundaries of how we understand and interpret the world around us.

CONTENTS

Dedicated to the Memory of Honorable Horace Davis of San Francisco as the only Tribute of Respect Now Possible to one whose Friendly Interest and Assistance the Author Here Gratefully Acknowledges

Up to the time of Starr King's death it was generally believed that he, more than any other man, had prevented California and the whole Pacific Coast from falling into the gulf of disunion. It is certain that Abraham Lincoln held this opinion

Edwin Percy Whipple

Introduction

This book is the result of the author's strong desire to know the truth relative to a critical period in the history of California, and a further strong desire to deal justly by the memory of a man recent historians have been pleased to pass by with slight acknowledgment.

What was the nature and measure of Starr King's influence on the Pacific Coast during the Civil War? To be able to answer that question has cost more time and study than the reader could be brought to believe. It has necessitated a thorough examination of all published histories of California, of numerous biographies, of old newspapers, memoirs, letters and musty documents. It has involved interviews with prominent persons as well as a careful study of earlier writings upon Starr King in books and magazines. Best of all it has compelled the writer to the delightful task of renewing his acquaintance with the published sermons and lectures of the patriot-preacher.

It is believed that no important data has been overlooked, and it is hoped that a genuine service has been rendered to all students of California History, and to all lovers of Starr King—he who was called by his own generation, "The Saint of the Pacific Coast."

Part I
In Old New England

When Starr King entered the Golden Gate, April 28, 1860, he had passed by a few months his thirty-fifth birthday. A young man in the morning of his power he felt strangely old, for he wrote to a friend just a little later: "I have passed meridian. It is after twelve o'clock in the large day of my mortal life. I am no longer a young man. It is now afternoon with me, and the shadows turn toward the east."

There was abundant reason for this premature feeling of age. Even at thirty-five King had been a long time among the most earnest of workers. Born in New York City, December 17, 1824, of English and German ancestry, son of a Universalist Minister who was compelled to struggle along on a very meager salary, the lad felt very early in life labor's stern discipline. At fifteen he was obliged to leave school that by daily toil he might help to support his now widowed mother and five younger brothers and sisters. Brief as was his record in school, we note the following prophetic facts: he displayed singular aptitude for study, he was conscientious yet vivacious, he was by nature adverse to anything rude or coarse. Joshua Bates, King's last teacher, describes the lad as "slight of build, golden haired, with a homely face which everybody thought handsome on account of the beaming eyes, the winning smile and the earnest desire of always wanting to do what was best and right."

This is our earliest testimony to the lovable character of the man whose life-story we are now considering. It will impress us more and more as East and West, Boston and San Francisco, in varying phrase tell again and again, of "the beaming eyes, the winning smile, and the earnest desire of always wanting to do what was just and right."

A bread-winner at fifteen, and for a large family, surely this is the end of all dreams of scholarship or of professional service. That depends on the man—and the conditions that surround him. Happily King's mother was a woman of good mind who knew and loved the best in literature. Ambitious for her gifted son, she read with him, and for him, certain of the masters whom to know well is to possess the foundations of true culture. It is a pretty scene and suggestive—the lad and his mother, reading together "till the wee small hours" Plutarch, Grote's History of Greece, Bullfinch's Mythology, Dante and the plays of William Shakespeare. Fortunately his mother was not his only helper. Near at hand was Theodore Parker who was said to possess the best private library in Boston, and whose passion for aiding young men was well known. He befriended King as he befriended others, and early discovered in the widow's son superior talents. In those days very young men used to preach. Before he had reached his majority, King was often sent to fill engagements under direction and at the suggestion of Parker. The high esteem of the elder for the younger man is attested by the following letter to an important church not far from Boston.

"I cannot come to preach for you as I would like, but with your kind permission I will send Thomas Starr King. This young man is not a regularly ordained preacher, but he has the grace of God in his heart, and the gift of tongues. He is a rare sweet spirit and I know that after you have met with him you will thank me for sending him to you."

This young dry-goods clerk, schoolmaster, and bookkeeper, for he followed all of these occupations during the years in which he was growing out of youth into manhood, was especially interested in metaphysics and theology. In these, and kindred studies he was greatly impressed and inspired by the writings of Victor Cousin, whose major gift was his ability to awaken other minds. "The most brilliant meteor that flashed across the sky of the nineteenth century," said Sainte-Beuve.

When Thomas Starr King was eighteen years old, William Ellery Channing died. Of that death which occurred amid the lovely scenery of Vermont upon a rare Autumnal evening, Theodore Parker wrote, The sun went toward the horizon: the slanting beams fell into the chamber. Channing turned his face toward that sinking orb and he and the sun went away together. Each, as the other, left "the smile of his departure' spread on all around: the sun on the clouds, he on the heart."

Channing's "smile on the heart," his pure philosophy, his sweet Christian spirit so influenced King that his best sermons read not unlike the large, calm utterances of Channing when he spoke on the loftiest of themes. To other good and great men our student preacher was deeply indebted. To Dr. Hosea Ballou (2d) for friendship and wise counsel. To Dr. James Walker for the inspiration of certain notable lectures on Natural Theology. Most of all to Dr. E. A. Chapin, his father's successor in the Universalist Pulpit at Charlestown, Mass. Dr. Chapin—but ten years King's senior—was then just beginning his eminent career as pulpit orator and popular lecturer. He recognized the undeveloped genius of his young friend, he knew of his earnest student-ship, he delighted to open the doors of opportunity to him. It was a gracious and honorable relation and most advantageous to the younger man. Writing to a good Deacon of a neighboring church Chapin said: "Thomas has never attended a Divinity School, but he is educated just the same. He speaks Greek, Hebrew, French, German, and fairly good English as you will see. He knows natural history and he knows humanity, and if one knows man and nature, he comes pretty close to knowing God."

In 1846 Chapin was called to New York, and through his influence Starr King, then twenty-two years old, was installed as his successor in the pastorate of the First Universalist Church of Charlestown. If his preparedness for an important New England pulpit is questioned it must be admitted that he entered it wholly without academic training, but we need not be distressed on that account. From the first he had adopted a method of study certain to produce excellent results, thorough acquaintance with a few great authors, and reverent, loving intercourse with a few great teachers. Little wonder that the "boy preacher" made good in the pulpit from which his honored Father had passed into, the Silence, and wherein the eloquence of Chapin had charmed a congregation of devoted followers.

Two years pass and he is called to Hollis Street Church in Boston, a Unitarian Church of honorable fame but at the time threatened with disaster. It was believed that if any one could save the imperilled church, King was that man. Not yet twenty-five years of age, established as minister of one of Boston's well known churches; a co-laborer of Bartol, Ballou, Everett, Emerson, Theodore Parker and Wendell Phillips,—surely he is to be tried and tested as few men so young have ever been, here in the "Athens of America," the city of beautiful ideals and great men.

It is certain that King regarded the eleven years he gave to Hollis Street as merely preparatory to his greater work in California. Writing playfully from San Francisco to Dr. Bellows in Boston he said: "At home, among you big fellows, I wasn't much. Here they seem to think I am somebody. Nothing like the right setting." The record shows that even among the "big fellows" Starr King was a very definite somebody, for although crowds did not attend his preaching in Boston as in San Francisco, he was able to congratulate himself upon the fact that he preached his last sermon in Hollis Street Church to five times as many people as heard his first. Nor do we need to await the judgment of California admirers to be convinced of his ability as a preacher or his popularity as a lecturer. It was said of him that "he was an orator from the beginning;" that his first public address "was like Charles Lamb's roast pig, good throughout, no part better or worse than another." "His delivery," says a candid and scholarly critic, "was rather earnest than passionate. He had a deep, strange, rich voice, which he knew how to use.

His eyes were extraordinary, living sermons, a peculiar shake and nod of the head giving the impression of deep-settled conviction. Closely confined to his notes, yet his delivery produces a marked impression."

Hostile criticism, which no man wholly escapes, enjoyed suggesting that King had been educated in the common schools of Portsmouth and Charlestown, and that he had graduated from the navy yard into the pulpit. A Boston correspondent passed judgment upon him as follows: "He was not considered profoundly learned; he was not regarded as a remarkable orator; he was not a great writer; nor can his unrivalled popularity be ascribed to his fascinating social or intellectual gifts. It was the hidden interior man of the heart that gave him his real power and skill to control the wills and to move the hearts, and to win the unbounded confidence and affection of his fellow-beings."

William Everett is authority for the statement that in those early years in Hollis Street Church "Starr King was not thought to be what a teacher of Boston Unitarianism ought to be. He was regarded rather as a florid platform speaker, one interested in the crude and restless attempts at reform which sober men distrusted." Another reviewer mingles praise and criticism quite ingeniously. "He astonishes and charms his hearers by a rare mastery over sentences. He is a skilful word-marshal. Hence his popularity as a lyceum lecturer. However much of elegant leisure the more solid and instructive lecturers may have, Mr. King is always wanted. He is, in some respects, the most popular writer and preacher of the two denominations which he equally represents, being a sort of soft ligament between the Chang of Universalism and the Eng of Unitarianism."

This last criticism invites us to notice—all too briefly—a phase of King's experience in New England fitting him most admirably for the larger work he was to do on the Pacific Coast. From 1840 to 1860 the Lyceum flourished in the United States as never before or since. Large numbers of lecture courses, extending even to the small cities and towns, were liberally patronized and generously supported. In many communities this was the one diversion and the one extravagance. To fill the new demand an extraordinary group of public speakers appeared; Emerson, Edward Everett, Wendell Phillips, Dr. Chapin, Oliver Wendell Holmes, George William Curtis, Henry Ward Beecher, Frederick Douglas, Theodore Parker and others, whose names are reverently spoken to this day by aged men and women who remember the uplift given them in youth by these giants of the platform.

That he was always wanted with such rivals as those is proof enough of King's power with the people, of his fame as an orator, even before his greater development and his more wonderful achievements in California.

His lecture circuit extended from Boston to Chicago. His principal subjects were "Goethe," "Socrates," "Substance and Show," a lecture which ranks next to Wendell Phillips' "Lost Arts" in popularity. Not withstanding the academic titles King gave his lectures they seemed to have been popular with all classes. "Grand, inspiring, instructive, lectures," said the learned. "Thems' idees," said unlettered men of sound sense. It was thought to be a remarkable triumph of platform eloquence that King could make such themes fascinating to Massachusetts farmers and Cape Cod fishermen. In fine phrase it was said of him that he lectured upon such themes as Plato and Socrates "with a prematureness of scholarship, a delicacy of discernment, a sweet innocent combination of confidence and diffidence, which were inexpressibly charming."

It may be claimed with all candor that few public teachers have ever been able so to enlist scientific truth in the service of the spirit. That spirit and life are the great realities, that all else is mainly show, at best but the changing vesture of spirit, is set forth in King's lectures so completely that he may be said to have made, even at this early age, a genuine and lasting contribution to the thought of his time. All this be it noted before he had set foot upon the Pacific Coast, where he was destined to do his real work.

One other service King had rendered the country, and especially New England, should here be gratefully recalled. Always in delicate health, he had formed the habit of spending his vacations in the White Hills of New Hampshire. Benefited in mind and body, and charmed by the rare beauty of a region then unknown, he endeavored to reveal to the people of Boston, and other Eastern cities, the neglected loveliness lying at their very doors. The result was King's "The White Hills, Their Legends, Landscape and Poetry." Although this pioneer nature-book is now probably quite forgotten, even by the multitudes who visit the scenes it so glowingly describes, it is well to remember that it was, indeed, one of the first attempts to entice the city dweller "back to nature." Published in 1859, it followed Thoreau's at that time unread "Walden" by only five years, while it preceded Murray's "Adventures in the Wilderness," and the earliest of John Burroughs' delightful volumes, by a full generation. It was in every way a commendable, if not great, adventure in authorship.

From this brief review it is evident that when Starr King preached his last sermon in Boston, March 25, 1860, he had made for himself an enviable reputation in three difficult fields of work, as preacher, lecturer and writer. The feeling of Boston and New England upon his departure was fittingly expressed by Edwin Percy Whipple in a leading journal of the day in which this eminent author "appealed to thousands in proof of the assertion that though in charge of a large parish, and with a lecture parish which extended from Bangor to St. Louis, he still seemed to have time for every noble work, to be open to every demand of misfortune, tender to every pretension of weakness, responsive to every call of sympathy, and true to every obligation of friendship; all will indulge the hope that California, cordial as must be the welcome she extends him, will still not be able to keep him long from Massachusetts."

On the day before he sailed from New York a "Breakfast Reception" was given him at the Fifth Avenue Hotel, at which three hundred guests were seated at the tables. The poet, William Cullen Bryant presided, and other men hardly less distinguished testified to the nature of King's work, and to the varied charm of his unique personality. Best of all, perhaps, was the tribute of his friend and neighbor, Dr. Frederick H. Hedge. "Happy Soul! himself a benediction wherever he goes; a living evangel of kind affections, better than all prophecy and all knowledge, the Angel of the Church whom Boston sends to San Francisco."

Such was the man who came to California in the greatest crisis of her history to exert upon her destiny an influence unequalled and unexampled even in that most romantic and eventful story of the Golden West.

Part II
California in 1860

The federal census of 1860 gave California 379,984 inhabitants and San Francisco 56,802. Historian Bancroft informs us that here was "a gathering without a parallel in history." It may be said that the whole history and development of California is without parallel. The story reads not so much like the orderly growth of a civilized community as a series of unrelated and episodical events. There is little of logical order or sequence, and much of surprise, adventure, of conflict and crisis. Said an aged philosopher, "It is the unexpected that happens," a saying illustrated if anywhere in the world, in the history of the Golden State.

Although discovered early in the sixteenth century by adventurous Spaniards, no serious attempt was made at settlement of any portion of the territory now included in the boundaries of California until the year 1769, when Father Junipero Serra arrived at the Bay of San Diego. Then followed a half century constituting the Mission Period of California history, during which Spanish Governors and Franciscan Friars ruled the land. Inspired more by religious zeal than by lust of conquest, or hope of gain, the Spanish Padres planted a chain of missions extending from San Diego to the Bay of San Francisco. At these missions, consisting often, at the beginning, of nothing more than a rude cross and altar, with some miserable make-shift of tent or huts as protection from the heat of summer and the cold of winter, the faithful priests labored to convert the surrounding Indians. They tried to make of them not alone good Catholics, but good farmers, and vineyardists, and according to the need of the time, capable carpenters and builders. As the result of their labors a long period of simple prosperity was enjoyed at the missions. Buildings were erected that still delight the traveler. They were for the most part of Moorish architecture, built of adobe, painted white, with red-tile roofs, long corridors and ever the secluded plaza where the friar might tell his beads in peace. Around the missions, some twenty in number, lying a day's journey apart between the southern and the central bay, Indian workers cultivated immense fields of grain, choice vineyards, olive orchards and orange groves; great herds of horses, cattle, and sheep were cared for, and the women became adept at weaving and spinning.

Nor were the Spanish Governors idle. They encouraged the immigration of settlers both from the mother country and Mexico by a most liberal policy, assisting the newcomer to build a home, acquire stock, and establish himself in a country where there was an abundance of game, and where the earth yielded her bounty with the minimum of labor. Thus in the half century between 1770 and 1820, these Pius Padres laid the foundations of California, as they believed securely, after Catholic and Spanish tradition.

Not securely so it proved, for in 1822 Mexico won her independence from Spain, both political and religious. The California Padres being Spaniards naturally suffered persecution at the hands of successive Mexican Governors, who were envious of the lands, orchards and herds of domestic animals belonging to the various missions. Ruthlessly the Friars were plundered of their well tilled fields, their fine vineyards, their flocks and herds, and their Indian converts were enticed or driven into the service of the new Masters of the country. Some of these officials were of Spanish blood and some of Mexican but now they proudly called themselves, Californians. And proudly they lived, these Spanish and Mexican Dons. Owning immense tracts of land, riding upon fleet horses, relieved of all necessity of honest work, they soon became in their manner of living, veritable hidalgoes.

Vain, ridiculously boastful, pleasure chasers, they loved above all else the frolic, the dance, and a good horse. All the way from San Diego to Shasta were located the immense ranchoes, more than six hundred in number, ever since celebrated in song and story. This was the period so often called by poetic writers the Romantic Age of California. Although much of the glamor of the dear old days of plenty and pleasure has been dispelled by the careful researches of conscientious scholars, it must still be admitted that here also were developed certain characteristics and here a kind of foundation for the future laid, ignorant of which we can not understand either the California of 1860 or even the State as we of today know and love it. If it is true that the first settlers in any community leave a lasting impress upon after generations it is evident that the Franciscan and Spanish background of California must be reviewed as we approach the more serious days of American conflict and conquest.

Although the first American settler arrived in California in 1816 his example seems to have been without effect for in 1822 there were but fourteen persons not of Mexican or Spanish blood in all the province. In the early '40's emigrants from the "States" began to come in parties, but so slowly that by January 1, 1848, the entire population (not including Indians) numbered only 14,000, and Yerba Buena (San Francisco) the only Pueblo of any size contained barely 900 inhabitants. This be it noted was but twelve years before the arrival of Starr King, so close was the old aristocratic rule of Spain to that stirring conflict in which he was to become a central figure.

As we have already observed it is the unexpected that happens in California history. In this same month of January, 1848, gold was discovered in the upper Sacramento Valley, an event that rivals the discovery of America by Columbus, if regarded in the light of results affecting the development of modern society. "The Gold that Drew the World" so Edwin Markham heads his story of that strange hegira which converted far-away California into a new Mecca and made of San Francisco, that sleepy Spanish Pueblo, in a few months' time a cosmopolitan city of fifty thousand people. Two years earlier, as a result of the Mexican War, California had been declared an American Territory, though not formally ceded to the United States until February 2, 1848. It was generally believed that the Mexican War had been waged and California acquired in the interest of negro slavery. James Russell Lowell voices this belief in the Bigelow papers as follows:

"They just wanted this California
So's to lug new slave states in,
To abuse ye and to scorn ye,
And to plunder ye like sin."

However this may have been, it is certain that among the immigrants of the fifty's there was a large number of forceful and brilliant men, loving the old South, and fully determined to swing the new state into line as a pro-slavery asset. It is true they were not strong enough to prevent the adoption in 1849 of a constitution prohibiting slavery, yet for all that, as Southern men they rejoiced when September 9, 1850, California was admitted to the Union.

It is no part of our purpose to give in detail the strange story of California during her first ten years as an American Commonwealth. By 1850 her population had increased to 120,000 people, mostly young men drawn by the lure of gold from every quarter of the civilized world, including not less than 4000 Chinese. Yet the majority were Americans, and of the Americans the larger number were from the slave states. Nor was this condition much altered up to the outbreak of the Civil War. Trustworthy authorities estimate that not less than forty per cent of her entire population were at that time of Southern birth, naturally Democratic in politics and for the most part pro-slavery in sentiment. It should be remembered that during the decade under consideration the national government was under the brilliant leadership of the slave-masters who were ever alert as to the attitude of this new Eldorado of the West. Consequently every position of trust and honor under national control in California was given to "safe men" whose attitude towards the "peculiar institution" was favorable beyond suspicion. To such an extent was this a matter of public knowledge that the Customs Station of San Francisco was popularly dubbed the "Virginia Poor House." During all these years California was under the absolute control of the Democratic Party, and the party was under control of its Pro-slavery leaders.

"The common people," says a late historian, "stood in awe for many years of these suave, urbane, occasionally fire-eating and always well-dressed gentlemen from this most aristocratic section of the Union. The Southerners, born leaders of men, and with politics the paramount interest in their lives, controlled both San Francisco and California."

J. W. Forney, a politician and reporter of the time, is more emphatic and declares that "California was a secession rendezvous from the day it became a part of the Union."

That the State was strongly Southern in sympathy is proven by the fact that of fifty-three newspapers published within her borders only seven advocated the election of Lincoln to the Presidency in 1860. A stronger proof still is found in the character and conduct of the public men of California during all the period under consideration. With one or two exceptions, of whom honorable mention later, every official of any importance, state or national, favored the South and voted in her interest. This condition was partly due, without doubt, to the political leadership of Senator Wm. M. Gwin. A Tennessean by birth, he was forty-six years of age, when he landed in San Francisco, June 4, 1849. Almost immediately active in politics he became the most brilliant and unscrupulous leader California has ever had. He held the reins of power and of national patronage until the war brought chaos to the old order and always Wm. M. Gwin was a faithful servant of the old aristocratic South of John C. Calhoun. He was ably seconded in his efforts to hold California to the pro-slavery cause by David S. Terry, Chief Justice of the State, and a fiery Texan, fearless and fierce in every conflict which might affect adversely Southern Chivalry. After these distinguished leaders there followed in monotonous succession Senators, Representatives, Governors, Legislators, representing doubtless their constituents in opposition to every movement looking to the abolition, or even serious limitation of the slave power.

The first man to challenge the almost solid cohorts of pro-slavery Democracy in California was David C. Broderick, United States Senator from 1857 until his untimely death in 1859. Broderick was the son of a stone cutter and in early life followed his father's trade. Born in Washington, D. C., he grew to manhood in New York City. When only twenty-six years old he became "Tammany's candidate for Congress." He was defeated and in June, 1849, he too arrived in San Francisco, determined never to return East unless as United States Senator. Plunging into the political life of the state as a loyal Democrat he was sent almost at once to the legislature in Sacramento, where he speedily became an influential member. In 1851 he was made presiding officer of the Senate and by 1852 his leadership within the State was so firmly established that it was said of him "he is the Democratic Party of California." January 10, 1857, after years of bitter struggle, Broderick was elected United States Senator, and the following March was duly received as a member of that august body. From the first his had been a strenuous career, he had been the storm center of heated contests, personal and political, in which he had commanded the suffrages of his fellows so completely that it was said, "men of all ages followed him like dogs." He had made many bitter and unrelenting enemies, and now that he had reached the goal of his ambition, he was to enter upon a last dread battle, the most severe and deadly of all he had known.

Stripped of all misleading complications the question then agitating Congress and the country was simply this: Shall Negro Slavery be forced upon the new territory of Kansas against the will of a majority of her people? This, of course, was only preliminary to the larger question: Shall the National Government, under lead of the Slave Oligarchy, be given power to spread over new territory, at will, the blight and curse of human bondage? Upon this foremost question of the day, Senator Broderick stood side by side with Stephen A. Douglas in opposition to the Buchanan Administration, and its mad attempt to force slavery upon the people of the New West. The attitude of California politicians on this matter is evidenced by the fact that the legislature in session at Sacramento promptly instructed Broderick to vote for the administration program, and a later legislature condemned him by resolution for failing to comply with the instructions of its predecessor and declared that his attitude was a disgrace and humiliation to the Nation. They demanded his immediate resignation. Let it be noted clearly that Broderick was condemned, not for opposing negro slavery, but simply and solely for opposing the extreme southern contention. Not long, however, was Broderick permitted to display his antislavery sympathies. During the exciting campaign of 1859, David S. Terry, believing himself aggrieved because of certain utterances of Broderick, challenged the latter to deadly combat. Reluctantly, but thereto compelled by long usage in California, Broderick met Terry upon the so-called "field of honor," September 13, 1859. Three days later Broderick was dead, a sacrifice, so all forward-looking men believed, to the wrath of the slave power. "His death was a political necessity, poorly veiled beneath the guise of a private quarrel." This was said at his funeral, and widely accepted among the people. It has been claimed that the death of Broderick saved California to the Union; that the revulsion of feeling following his bloody death was so great that his beloved State became good soil for the new teaching of Lincoln and the Republican Party. Generously one would like to accept this theory were not the evidence so strongly against it. To Broderick belongs the high honor of inaugurating the fight on the Pacific Coast against the extension of slavery. In the outset of that conflict he perished, and the manner of his taking off gave to his message something of the force of martyrdom. But not to the extent his admirers have imagined. It should be clearly noted that Broderick believed in local self-government regarding slavery. He believed that the people of Kansas, and the people of Virginia (as of all other states) possessed the right under our national constitution, of deciding this question for themselves without let or hindrance by the general government. Farther than this he did not go. To the day of his death, he was a loyal Douglas Democrat. It should be further noted that in this last campaign of Broderick's life the pro-slavery Democracy swept the State, its candidate for Governor being elected by a vote nearly twice the combined vote of the Douglas and Republican candidates: And, also, that a year after Broderick's death Abraham Lincoln polled only twenty-eight per cent of the popular vote in California for President of the United States. Whatever may have been the influence of the Senator's brave conflict in Congress, or his untimely death, it is evident that the crisis in California's attitude toward the Union had not yet arrived, that the hour in which any man might change the course of events still lay within the unknown future.

The same may be said of the life and work of a still more brilliant opponent of slavery on this Coast, Col. Edward D. Baker, a man of phenomenal eloquence, with a well earned reputation as a successful lawyer and politician, with an honorable record for gallant service in the Mexican War, and for useful service in the House of Representatives in Washington. When he located in San Francisco in 1852, an immigrant from the great State of Illinois, he brought new strength to the minority who were in conscience opposed to the growing dominion of the Slave Power. For certain reasons, well understood at the time and which do not concern us here, Col. Baker did not wield the influence which his talents would naturally have secured for him. Yet as the contest deepened, his majestic eloquence was beyond question a force for freedom in a community where the love of oratory amounted to a passion. In the Fremont Campaign, at the grave of Broderick, and in his own canvass for Congress in 1859, he rendered most valuable service in laying the foundations of Republicanism on the Pacific Coast. But it should be remembered by all who would deal with those great days fairly that the work of Edward Dickinson Baker at its best was only the work of a brilliant forerunner. Before the real battle was on he removed from the State, and as the newly elected United States Senator from Oregon, from this Coast. It is true that on his journey to Washington a few days before the National election in November, 1860, Baker delivered in San Francisco an effective speech on Lincoln's behalf, but it is foolish hero-worship to say, of California! Not only had Baker been defeated overwhelmingly a few months earlier as Republican candidate for Congress, but Lincoln himself received the electoral vote of California only as the result of a three-sided contest in which the combined opposition polled nearly three-fourths of all the votes cast. In fact Lincoln distanced his nearest Democratic rival by only 711 Votes. Out of one hundred and fourteen members of the state legislature but twenty-four belonged to the party of Lincoln. The Congressional Delegation was solidly Democratic, and the Governor was a Southern sympathizer. Such was the condition after Baker's work was done in California, and when the greater work of Starr King was just beginning.

In justice to Colonel Baker, though it is no part of our duty here, we make grateful mention of the fact that not on the Pacific Coast but in Washington, as the friend and adviser of President Lincoln, and on the floor of the United States Senate, this gallant defender of Union and Liberty rendered a unique and memorable service to his country. His replies in the Senate to those giants of the Confederacy, John C. Breckenridge and Judah P. Benjamin attained the dignity of national events, and his heroic death early in the war on field of battle renders it forever impossible for any just man to belittle the deeds or influence of Edward D. Baker. What he might have effected had he remained in California, or had his life been longer spared, we may not say. The fact remains that after his mission among us was over Southern and Democratic sentiment was still in the ascendant. It was reserved for another,—the privilege and the honor of "saving California to the Union."

One other phase of the situation merits careful attention. Almost from the very beginning of American Settlement in California a dream of Pacific Empire, separate and independent of "the States" had fascinated many of her strongest men. And little wonder, for here by the Pacific Sea was a vast territory walled away by lofty mountains and wide deserts, two thousand miles west of the frontier settlements of Minnesota and Kansas. Not until after the outbreak of the Civil War was there telegraphic communication with the East, and the nearest railway ended somewhere in central Missouri. Mail was received regularly once in twenty-six days, sometimes as often as once in two weeks. But there was little direct communication and less unity of purpose between the older sections of the United States and far away California. In fact there was considerable antagonism felt and expressed toward the government of Washington. The original Mexican population cordially hated, and with good reason, the national authority. Foreigners in the mines cared nothing for the Union or the quarrel between the states, and many of the settlers from the East, which they still lovingly called "back home," felt that they had a real grievance against the general government. This feeling, which was of long standing, was naturally intensified by the troubled outlook in 1860. Men prominent in state and national politics openly advocated independence as the proper policy for the Pacific Coast.

"Why depend on the South or the North to regulate our affairs," wrote our junior Senator from Washington. "And this, too, after they have proved themselves incapable of living in harmony with one another." Starr King had been a resident of the state nearly a year when the San Francisco Herald published the following letter received from Congressman John C. Burch:

"The people of California should all be of one mind on this subject of a Pacific Republic. Raise aloft the flag of the hydraheaded cactus of the western wilds and call upon the enlightened nations of the earth to acknowledge our independence and protect us from the wreck of a once glorious Union."

Governor John B. Weller, a man not only holding the highest office within the gift of the people of the state, but also one who had represented California in the United States Senate made deliberately this declaration:

"If the wild spirit of fanaticism which now pervades the land should destroy the magnificent confederacy—which God forbid—California will not go with the south or north, but here on the shores of the Pacific, found a mighty republic, which may in the end prove the greatest of all."

These quotations which might be greatly extended are sufficient to prove that a strong feeling existed in favor of a Pacific Republic standing wholly aloof from the coming struggle. It is unthinkable that a Senator and a Congressman, and especially the Governor of the State, should have voiced such sentiments had there not been at least a probability that this might be the course adopted in case the Union was broken up.

James G. Blaine, whose history of the time must be regarded as impartial so far as California is concerned, makes this statement:

"Jefferson Davis expected, with confidence amounting to certainty, and based, it is believed, on personal pledges, that the Pacific Coast, if it did not actually join the South, would be disloyal to the Union."

This beyond reasonable doubt was the situation in the Spring of 1860: Our immense State with its coast line of more than seven hundred miles, sharply divided as between Southern and Northern California; the majority of our people in Los Angeles and neighboring counties frankly favoring the proposed confederacy of slave-holding states; many of the larger towns in the San Joaquin and Sacramento valleys of a similar mind; the political leaders of the State almost solidly Democratic and the majority with strong Southern leanings; many of our foremost men believing that the time had come to launch the long dreamed of Pacific Republic, and our ranches and mines containing a large population either hostile or indifferent to the cause of Union and Liberty. Over against these varied forces a probable patriotic majority scattered from one end of California to the other, some belonging to the new Republican Party and some to the Douglas Democracy, and many without party affiliation, unorganized, badly scattered, and now that Broderick was dead and Colonel Baker away, without competent leadership. If ever a situation called for a man who might at once command the confidence of the people and arouse the latent patriotism of our wide-spread population, a man who might do the work of years in a few months' time, who might in his own persuasive personality become a center of patriotism around which Union-loving men of all parties, and of no party, could unite in defense of the imperilled country; one unfettered by old antagonisms, or misled by personal ambition, a heaven-sent man destined to a work no other could accomplish—this the situation plainly demanded.

The record, impartially examined, shows, we believe beyond reasonable doubt, that California's destiny in this critical hour was chiefly determined by the word and work of her patriot-preacher, Starr King.

Part III
California's Hour of Decision

The period that determined California's attitude during the Civil War, coincides almost exactly with the first year and a half of Starr King's residence in the State. Less than a month after he had preached his first sermon in San Francisco, Abraham Lincoln received the presidential nomination at Chicago, and the great debate was on.

It should be remembered that King's reputation as a lecturer had preceded him, and that he was hardly settled in his new home before he was flooded with invitations to lecture here as he had done in the East. As soon as possible, and as far as possible, he accepted these invitations regarding them as calls to service in the interest of an enlightened patriotism. Choosing as subjects such themes as "Washington," "Webster," "Lexington and Concord," he made of them all a plea for a united country, one glorious land from Maine to the Sierras. He seems to have perceived the danger hidden in the perfectly natural ambition of leading men to take advantage of the troubled time to launch the Pacific Republic, and thus avoid all danger of the coming conflict between North and South. A free, independent California, which should practically include the entire Coast,—surely here was an inspiring and seductive dream. By a method peculiarly his own he did not directly combat this fascinating idea, but rather sought to win his hearers to the larger vision of an empire extending from ocean to ocean, every mile of it dedicated to liberty and progress.

"What a privilege it is to be an American," he exclaims in a favorite lecture, often repeated.

"Suppose that the continent could turn towards you tomorrow at sunrise, and show to you the whole American area in the short hours of the sun's advance from Eastport to the Pacific! You would see New England roll into light from the green plumes of Aroostook to the silver stripe of the Hudson; westward thence over the Empire State, and over the lakes, and over the sweet valleys of Pennsylvania, and over the prairies, the morning blush would run and would waken all the line of the Mississippi; from the frosts where it rises, to the fervid waters in which it pours, for three thousand miles it would be visible, fed by rivers that flow from every mile of the Allegheny slope, and edged by the green embroideries of the temperate and tropic zones; beyond this line another basin, too, the Missouri, catching the morning, leads your eye along its western slope till the Rocky Mountains burst upon the vision, and yet do not bar it; across its passes we must follow, as the stubborn courage of American pioneers has forced its way, till again the Sierra and their silver veins are tinted along the mighty bulwark with the break of day; and then over to the gold-fields of the western slope, and the fatness of the California soil, and the beautiful valleys of Oregon, and the stately forests of Washington, the eye is drawn, as the globe turns out of the night-shadow, and when the Pacific waves are crested with radiance, you have the one blending picture, nay, the reality, of the American domain! No such soil, so varied by climate, by products, by mineral riches, by forest and lake, by wild heights and buttresses, and by opulent plains,—yet all bound into unity of configuration and bordered by both warm and icy seas,—no such domain was ever given to one people."

In many communities and in varying phrase—always earnest and eloquent—King returned to the central theme of all his thinking and speaking, the greatness and glory of the Union,—"one and indivisible." The following but illustrates the constant tenor of his teaching:

"If all that the past has done for us and the present reveals could stand apparent in one picture, and then if the promise of the future to the children of our millions under our common law, and with continental peace, could be caught in one vast spectral exhibition, the wealth in store, the power, the privilege, the freedom, the learning, the expansive and varied and mighty unity in fellowship, almost fulfilling the poet's dream of

'The Parliament of man, the federation of the world,'

you would exclaim with exultation, 'I, too, am an American!' You would feel that patriotism, next to your tie to the Divine Love, is the greatest privilege of your life; and you would devote yourselves, out of inspiration and joy, to the obligations of patriotism, that this land so spread, so adorned, so colonized, so blessed, should be kept forever, against all the assaults of traitors, one in polity, in spirit, and in aim!"

In a way we may say that King found himself in these first months in California. He was forced by the number of his engagements, as well as by the more direct demands of a new country, to throw aside his manuscripts, and, making such preparation as conditions would permit, launch boldly out upon the dangerous sea of extempore speech. He was constantly addressing audiences in whole, or in part, hostile. Writing to an Eastern friend of his experiences in the Sacramento Valley, he says, "You see in glaring capitals,

'Texas Saloon,' 'Mississippi Shoe Shop,' 'Alabama Emporium.' Very rarely do you see any Northern state thus signalized." Men of substance, natural leaders of the people, were in most communities either for Breckenridge or Douglas. The man was grappling with the intellectual soldiery of disunion. The same forces that had transformed Lincoln, the Illinois politician into a national figure, the standard bearer of a great party, were working upon King. And the same method which caused Horace Greeley to write of Lincoln, "He is the greatest Convincer of his day" was followed by the younger patriot, face to face as he was with incipient disloyalty. He was accustomed, even as Lincoln, to state his opponent's argument fully and fairly, and then without unnecessary severity, demolish it. An old miner, listening to one of Starr King's patriotic speeches, delighting in the intellectual dexterity displayed, exclaimed, "Boys, watch him, he is taking every trick." The necessity of "taking every trick," and this so far as possible without offence, quickened his powers and led to the full development of his many sided eloquence.

How he was regarded during these early months when he had literally plunged into the life of a community where nothing was as yet fixed, where everything was in the making, where the most serious questions of duty and destiny were stirring the hearts and consciences of men, — is made clear to us by the testimony of contemporaries whose sole desire must have been to render honor where honor was due.

The latest and most complete history of California based upon the most trustworthy evidence extant gives cautious tribute to the Starr King of this period as follows:

"The Republicans had lost their most effective orator since the campaign of the preceding year, Colonel Baker, but his loss was in some degree compensated for by the appearance of an unheralded but equally eloquent speaker, Thomas Starr King, who arrived in April, 1860, and later toured the state, giving lectures on patriotic subjects but always declared for the Union and the Republican candidates as the surest guaranty of its preservation."

Tuthill, in his history of the time writes with more warmth, and probably more truth:

"There was a charm in King's delivery that few could resist. He was received with applause where Republican orators, saying things no more radical, could not be heard without hisses. Delicately feeling his way, and never arousing the prejudices of his hearers, he adroitly educated his audiences to a lofty style of patriotism. The effect was obvious in San Francisco where audiences were accustomed to every style of address; it was far more noticeable in the interior."

The celebrated critic and writer, Edwin Percey Whipple, made a careful examination of King's record in California and sums up his impressions as follows:

"As a patriotic Christian statesman he included the real elements of power in the community, took the people out of hands of disloyal politicians, lifted them up to the level of his own ardent soul, and not only saved the state to the Union, but imprinted his own generous and magnanimous spirit on its forming life."

Writing a little later and with even more enthusiasm, another authority, speaking of King's charm of manner, says:

"I am persuaded that could he have gone through the Southern states, shaking hands with secessionists, he would have won them back to their allegiance by the mere magnetism of his touch."

It is, perhaps, impossible at this late date to estimate the effect of Starr King's appeal to the voters of California in the presidential election of 1860. As we have already noted, Lincoln carried the State by a very narrow plurality, and we need not ascribe the swaying of many votes to the eloquence of King's advocacy to make it appear that his influence was marked in that memorable campaign.

But here must be emphasized a fact, quite often overlooked, and always to the serious perversion of history. In California, as in every doubtful state, the Hour of Decision did not precede, but in every instance, followed the elevation of Lincoln to the presidency. It was upon this rock that the nation split. Shall a Black Republican be permitted to sit in the seat of Washington? Shall a man elected, as a matter of fact, by a sectional minority rule over Virginia—mother of Presidents—over imperial Texas, or the Golden West? To us the case seems clear. Abraham Lincoln, who commanded 180 votes in the electoral college to 123 divided among his opponents, was by our constitution President-elect of the United States. To the men of that day the case was by no means settled. The national bond was weak. The local, or state bond was strong. It was a time of intense political passion. The irrepressible conflict which had clouded the closing days of Henry Clay and Daniel Webster must now be decided, either for, or against, the extension of human slavery; either for, or against, a National Union.

Well meaning, but mistaken, writers have claimed that California was never a doubtful state, that the great majority of her people were ever loyal to the Northern cause, to Lincoln and Liberty. As a matter of sober truth let it be here written that the attitude of no state north of Mason and Dixon's Line gave Northern leaders so grave concern. Nor was the matter once for all decided until the election of Leland Stanford in September, 1861, as the first Republican Governor of California. During all the Spring and Summer of that great year the battle waged with the issue, up to the last hour, uncertain. These were the months that tried men's souls in California, as in the Border States. Communities were divided. Party ties severed. Families broken up. Old friendships sundered. All lesser questions were lost sight of as Union, or Dis-union, became the all absorbing theme. The battle of ideas, preceding the battle of bullets, was on.

What was the state of public opinion in California? How runs the evidence?

In March, 1861, General E. V. Sumner was given command of United States regulars on the Pacific Coast, replacing Albert Sidney Johnston, whose well known attachment to the Southern cause led to his removal by the Lincoln Administration. In General Sumner's reports to the War Department in Washington we have impartial and official testimony as to conditions in California during the period under consideration. Naturally he came first in contact with the people about San Francisco Bay, a majority of whom were loyal to the North, and consequently, Sumner's first reports were encouraging. "There is a strong Union feeling," he writes, "with the majority of the people of the state, but the Secessionists are much the most active and zealous party."

A little later, better informed, he reported: "The Secessionist party in this state numbers about 32,000 men and they are very restless and zealous, which gives them great influence." Still later: "The disaffection in the southern part of the state is increasing and is becoming dangerous, and it is indispensably necessary to throw reinforcements into that section immediately."

In this connection it should be remembered that when President Lincoln at the outbreak of the war called for 75,000 men, California was expected to furnish her quota of 6,000 soldiers, but so threatening was the local situation that not a loyal man could be spared from the State. On the contrary it was found necessary to retain in the State certain regiments of the regular army badly needed elsewhere. In the summer of 1861, the War Department proposed to transfer a portion of the regular army stationed in California to Texas, where the situation demanded immediate succor for the friends of the Union. How grave the situation had become in California may easily be determined by a fact which seems to have escaped so far the attention of historians. On August 28, 1861, the leading men of San Francisco sent a communication to Hon. Simon Cameron, Secretary of War, remonstrating against the withdrawal of United States troops from California for the following reasons:

1. "A majority of our present state officials are avowed secessionists, and the balance being bitterly hostile to the administration are advocates of a peace policy at any price."

2. "About three-fifths of our citizens are natives of slave-holding states and are almost a unit in this crisis."

3. "Our advices, obtained with great prudence and care, show us that there are about 16,000 Knights of the Golden Circle (a secret military organization of secessionists, said by many authorities to have been much stronger than was at the time believed) in the state, and they are still organizing even in our most loyal districts."

4. "Through misrepresentation the powerful native Mexican population has been won over to the secession side."

This document, remarkable in itself, becomes weighty evidence, when it is stated that after full and careful consideration, the petition was heeded and the regulars remained on the Coast.

General Sumner held command nearly a year, until, as we are accustomed to think, all danger of a disloyal California was over, yet as the date of his departure for the Army of the Potomac drew near, he was very anxious that Col. Wright, an able and loyal officer, should fill his place, and wrote to the authorities in Washington, "Col. Wright ought to remain in command. The safety of the whole coast may depend upon it." (italics ours).

A few weeks after the death of Starr King, the Pacific Monthly, leading magazine of the day, reviewed the situation at the beginning of the great conflict, as it was then known and understood by all intelligent Californians:

"On the breaking out of the rebellion, public opinion on this coast was sorely distracted at the issues raised. The great majority of the people were warmly attached to their Government; but they had drunk deep at the fountains of Southern eloquence, and had been measurably debauched by the dangerous teachings of the able men who had ruled the state from its infancy. When we consider the critical condition of public sentiment at that dark hour (1860-1861); how the public mind had been thrown off its poise by the false teaching of a long succession of political charlatans; how the insidious doctrine of separation and a Pacific Republic had been hissed by serpents into the ears of the people; how the great dark cloud of impending ruin hung over our central Government; how legions of armed patricides were almost battering at the gates of our National Capital; how rebellion had baptized itself in blood and victory at Bull Run—when we think how the effect of all these adverse teachings and adverse fortunes had rendered the public mind plastic to whoever had the genius to seize and direct it, and reflect that a man of King's abilities, but without his patriotism, might have grasped the opportunity to drift us upon shoals and rocks and quicksands of treason, we cannot feel too thankful that the man and the hour both arrived. His was a noble task, and nobly did he fulfill it. What he did for California and the Union can never be fully estimated,—the work he wrought in saving her to the country, and engraving upon her heart, the golden word—'Union'."

Leaving aside for a little space this fervent tribute to King's work, the quotation just given is evidence of a grave situation, of a state divided in opinion, of just such an "hour of decision" as gives the strong man his opportunity. There can be no doubt that the verdict of the Visalia Delta, a loyal and well-known newspaper, as to conditions in its own community would apply to every considerable town in the State:

"Treason against the Government and constitution is preached from the pulpit, printed in the newspapers, and openly advocated in the streets and public places."

A work just from the press, "California—Men and Events"—by Mr. G. H. Tinkham, affords valuable testimony to the necessity and value of King's mission as patriotic leader:

"At a time when some Union men were paralyzed with dread, and others undecided which way to turn, Thomas Starr King traveled over the state bolstering up the weak-hearted, and urging loyal men to stand firmly for the Union. In his lectures, 'Washington,' 'Daniel Webster,' 'The Great Uprising,' and 'The Rebellion in Heaven,' in unanswerable arguments and matchless eloquence he kindled the patriotism of the people into a glowing flame. It is conceded that no individual did more to keep California in the Union than did Thomas Starr King."

How necessary it was that some one should "kindle the patriotism of the people into a glowing flame" is further evident from the fact that the California Legislature of 1861 numbered as its members 57 Douglas Democrats, 33 Southern Democrats, and but 24 Republicans. What this alignment signified may be judged from the following incident. Edmund Randolph, (a former Virginian, and a man of fiery eloquence) on July 11, 1861, delivered unrebuked in the State Democratic Convention at Sacramento, this diatribe against Abraham Lincoln: "For God's sake speed the ball, may the lead go quick to his heart—and may our country be free from this despot usurper, that now claims to the name of President of the United States."

A few days earlier, July 4, 1861, a Confederate flag waved undisturbed in Los Angeles, as well as in other nearby towns, the Union men in that section being largely in the minority. For a considerable time in the United States Marshal's office in San Francisco, a Confederate flag waved from a miniature man-of-war named "Jeff Davis."

In Merced County, Union men were in a sorry minority! A favorite campaign song in that region was entitled, "We'll Drive the Bloody Tyrant Lincoln From Our Dear Native Soil." A little later, the Equal Rights Expositer of Visalia characterized President Lincoln as "a narrow minded bigot, an unprincipled demagogue, and a drivelling, idiotic, imbecile creature."

Unpleasant testimony of this sort, demonstrating the presence and power of a bitter spirit of disloyalty, running all through the State, but most in evidence in certain localities peopled from the South, might be given at great length. But enough. We have no wish to reproduce the evil passions of an evil time further than to make it absolutely clear that a real danger of disunion existed, and that friend and foe alike recognized that, under God, the undaunted leader of Union sentiment in California was none other than Starr King.

A prominent San Francisco paper, indulging in the partizan speech of the period, calling all friends of the Administration at Washington, "Abolitionists," gave ungracious testimony to King's standing and influence as follows:

"The abolitionists are bent on carrying out their plans, and will not hesitate to commit any act of despotism. If the constitution stands in their way, they will, to use the words of their champion in this state, Rev. T. Starr King, drive through the constitution."

"Their champion in this state." The opprobrium rested upon him then; let the honor be his now. This in simple justice to the truth of history.

It is infinitely to be regretted that what men called "the irresistible charm of his eloquence" cannot by any manner of speech be here portrayed. If excuse is necessary let these words from King's lecture on "Webster" plead for us:

"Alas for the perishableness of eloquence! It is the only thing in the higher walks of human creativeness that passes away. The statue lives after the sculptor dies, as sublime as when his chisel left it. St. Peter's is a perpetual memorial and utterance of the great mind of Angelo. The Iliad is as fresh today as twenty-five centuries ago. The picture may grow richer with years. But great oratory, the most delightful and marvelous of the expressions of mortal power, passes and dies with the occasion."

Not wholly, for even in "cold type" some measure of the power and persuasiveness of the orator's argument is suggested. It is easy to imagine the force and fire of patriotism that must have glowed in such words as these:

"Rebellion sins against the Mississippi; it sins against the coast line; it sins against the ballot-box; it sins against oaths of allegiance; it sins against public and beneficent peace; and it sins, worse than all, against the cornerstone of American progress and history and hope,—the worth of the laborer, the rights of man. It strikes for barbarism against civilization."

The intense fervor of King's loyalty to Union and Liberty is seen in his righteous indignation against an Oregonian who would not fight to save the country unless he could be shown that his own personal interests were involved. "For one wild moment," wrote King, "I longed to throttle the wretch and push him into the Columbia. I looked down, however, and saw that the water was clean."

Think of the force of the following declaration uttered to men who meant well, but were undecided:

"The Rebellion—it is the cause of Wrong against Right. It is not only an unjustifiable revolution, but a geographical wrong, a moral wrong, a religious wrong, a war against the Constitution, against the New Testament, against God."

Thus did he condemn all forces within the State at war with liberty and right. Stern words he used,—words that like Luther's were half battles. Of peace-at-any-price-men he said:

"The hounds on the track of Broderick turned peace men, and affected with hysterics at the sniff of powder! Wonderful transformation. What a pleasant sight—a hawk looking so innocent, and preaching peace to doves, his talons loosely wound with cotton! A clump of wolves trying to thicken their ravenous flanks with wool, for this occasion only, and composing their fangs to the work of eating grass! Holy Satan, pray for us."

When the report reached California that Robert Toombs had said, "I want it carved over my grave,—'Here lies the man who destroyed the United States Government and its Capitol,'" King replied, "Mr. Toombs cannot be literally gratified. But he may come so near his wish as this,—that it shall be written over his gallows, as over every one of a score of his fellow-felons, 'Here swings the man who attempted murder on the largest scale that was ever planned in history.'"

That our orator knew how to be sarcastic as well as severe must have been plain to those who heard him exclaim:

"There are those who say that they are Union men, and in favor of the Government, and yet they are bitterly opposed to the administration, and cannot support its policy. But in a war for self existence, this divorce is impossible. One might as well say at a fire, while his house is beginning to crackle in the flames, 'I am in favor of this engine, I go for this water; the hose meets my endorsement. Certainly, I am for putting out the fire, but don't ask me to help man the brakes, for I am conscientiously opposed to the hose pipe. Its nozzle isn't handsome. It wasn't made by a Democrat.'"

How ardently King longed for the liberation of the Blacks is seen in the following, addressed in all probability more to the President of the United States than to the people:

"O that the President would soon speak that electric sentence,—inspiration to the loyal North, doom to the traitorous aristocracy whose cup of guilt is full! Let him say that it is a war of mass against class, of America against feudalism, of the schoolmaster against the slave-master, of workmen against the barons, of the ballot-box against the barracoon. This is what the struggle means. Proclaim it so, and what a light breaks through our leaden sky! The war-wave rolls then with the impetus and weight of an idea."

Closing his greatest patriotic lecture, most in demand by the public along the entire Coast, "Daniel Webster," Starr King quotes Webster's noble peroration in the "Reply to Hayne," "Liberty and Union, Now and Forever, One and Inseparable," and in lofty strain of patriotic prophecy announces that:

"Mr. Webster's thought breaks out afresh in the proclamation of the President that America is one and cannot be broken; it bursts forth in the banners thick as the gorgeous leaves of the October forests that have blossomed all over eighteen or twenty States; it shows itself in the passion of the noble Union men of the South who will not bow to Baal; it floats on every frigate that rides the sea to protect our shipping; it leaps forth and brightens in the sacred steel which patriots by the hundred thousand are dedicating, not to ravage, not to murder, not to hatred of any portion of the southern section of the confederacy, but to the support of the impartial Constitution, to the common flag, to the majestic and beneficent law which offers to encircle and bless the whole republic; it utters itself in the thunder-voice of twenty millions of white citizens of the land, that in America the majority under the Constitution must rule, and the public law must be obeyed.

"And when the work of the government shall be accomplished,—when the stolen money of the nation shall be refunded; when hostile artillery shall be with-drawn from the lower banks of the Mississippi; when the flag of thirteen stripes and thirty-four stars shall float again over Sumter, over New Orleans, over every arsenal that has seen it insulted, over Mount Vernon and the American dust of Washington, over every State Capitol and along the whole coast and border line of Texas; when every man within the present limits of the immense republic shall have restored to him the right of pride in the American Navy, and of representation on common terms in the National Capitol, and of citizenship on the whole continent; when leading traitors shall have been punished, and the Constitution vindicated in its unsectional beneficence, and the doctrine of secession be stabbed with two hundred thousand bayonet wounds, and trampled to rise no more,— then the debate between Mr. Calhoun and Mr. Webster will be completed, the swarthy spirit of the great defender of the Constitution will triumph, and a restored, peaceful, majestic, irresistible America will dignify and consecrate his name forever."

"A restored, peaceful, majestic, irresistible America,"—this was the vision that nerved King to herculean labor, to a most real martyrdom. Condemned to the slow suicide of over-work, he gave his life a conscious offering to freedom. "What a year to live in," he writes, "worth all other times ever known in our history or any other." Again,—"I should be broken down if I had time to think how I feel. I am beginning to look old, and shall break before my prime."

Why is the song so sweet, and why does it move us so strangely? The singer's heart is breaking. Why is the word so effective? It is laden with love and winged with sacrifice. A man is dying that others may live in verity, not longer in shadow; a hero is suffering crucifixion that the sad ages may a little change their course. Not only is it true that the "blood of martyrs slain is the seed of the church," but it is also true that a man never touches the heights of power until he has made a total, irreversible, affectionate surrender to the cause he professes to serve. When he has done this the cause becomes incarnate in the man; and he speaks as one inspired. And this was the power of Starr King in that great Summer and Fall of 1861 in California. Of course he did not speak in vain. Leland Stanford, backed by a Union Legislature, was elected Governor of California, and by October, King joyfully writing an Eastern friend was able to say "the State is safe from southern tampering."

Part IV
Philanthropist and Preacher

"As a philanthropist, Starr King raised for the most beneficent of all charities the most munificent of all subscriptions." These words were spoken at the King Memorial Service held in the city of Boston, April 3, 1864. They call our attention to a unique service our Preacher-Patriot rendered the cause he loved.

It seems almost beyond belief that the North rushed into the Civil War wholly unprepared to care for the Nation's Defenders, either in health or in sickness. Transportation facilities were of the poorest! Young men just from the home, the farm and the college were crowded into cattle cars as though they were beasts, frequently with no provision whatever for their comfort. And rarely were proper arrangements made for their reception in camp. The bewildered soldiers stood for hours under broiling southern sun, waiting for rations and shelter, while ignorant officers were slowly learning their unaccustomed duties. At night they were compelled to lie wrapped in shoddy blankets upon rotten straw. Under such conditions these brave volunteers suffered severely and camp diseases became alarmingly prevalent. But the miserable makeshifts used as hospitals were so bad that sick men fought for the privilege of dying in camp with their comrades rather than undergo the privations, and sometimes the brutality of inexperienced and careless attendants in the crowded and poorly equipped quarters provided by the government. The largest hospital available contained but forty beds, and not one afforded a trained, efficient, medical staff. Competent nurses, sanitary kitchens, proper medicines, means of humanely transporting the sick and wounded, all were wanting during early months of the war.

This condition which the government did almost nothing to remedy led to the organization of the United States Sanitary Commission. Strangely enough the founder of this most necessary and timely organization, Rev. H. W. Bellows, of New York, encountered the opposition of high officials who deemed the whole plan quixotic. Even President Lincoln at first regarded the Commission unnecessary and called it "a fifth wheel to the coach." Brief experience, however, demonstrated that the government could not provide all that was necessary for the soldier, either in sickness or in health, and the Sanitary Commission became often the only hope of brave men in dire distress. In fact, at this day, it is difficult to see how the Northern cause would have triumphed at all but for the widespread and wholly helpful activity of the army of Sanitary workers.

The greatest difficulty encountered by the leaders of this noble philanthropy was to provide necessary funds. Again and again it seemed that the work must stop because the heavily burdened people could give no more. At sundry critical junctures California came to the rescue, and made possible the continuance of this "most beneficent of all charities." But at whose motion, and under whose influence?

Fitz Hugh Ludlow says, "Starr King was the Sanitary Commission of California." This is but slight exaggeration, for King made it his peculiar mission to raise money as rapidly as possible for the suffering soldiers. In the interest of the Commission he traveled to every part of the Coast, and in the face of the greatest obstacles became the principal factor in raising $1,235,000, about one-fourth of the entire sum contributed by the country at large. Under the most favorable circumstances this would have been a phenomenal achievement, but when we learn that in 1862 a flood destroyed over fifty million dollars' worth of property in the Sacramento and San Joaquin valleys; that California shipping to the extent of six and one-half millions was also destroyed; that in 1863 a drought entirely ruined the wheat crop, and made hay so scarce that it sold for sixty dollars a ton, resulting in a stagnation in business which threw thousands of men out of employment, in view of these multiplied disasters, we wonder by what fire of patriotism and by what charm of eloquence, Starr King drew from the people so large a sum for use on distant battle fields. Old Californians still remember those thrilling appeals which few could resist. We are almost led to believe in the sober truth of such extreme eulogy as we find in "Lights and Shadows of the Pacific Coast," by S. D. Woods, a venerable San Franciscan, who vividly recalls King's heroic service in that far off time:

"King's personality was magnetic and winning. Gentleness radiated from him as light radiates from the sun. No one could resist the charm and fascination of his presence. It is hard to make a pen picture of his face, for there were lines too pure, lights too fleeting to be caught by words. In the poise of his head there was nobility and power inexpressible. There was in his face the serenity of one who had seen a vision, and to whom the vision had become a benediction. At the time of his death he was the first pulpit orator in America, and without doubt had no superior in the world."

This large praise might lead to incredulity were it not for the deliberate judgment of Rev. Dr. H. W. Bellows, that as an orator "Beecher and Chapin were his only competitors. He was the admirer and friend of both, and both repaid his affection and his esteem. He had the superior charm of youth and novelty, with a nature more varied, and more versatile faculties and endowments than either. He had a far more artistic and formative nature and genius. His thoughts ran into moulds of beauty."

The judgment of California as to Starr King's unequalled service to the State and the Nation was officially rendered when upon the announcement of his death, the Legislature adjourned for the space of three days after resolving "that he had been a tower of strength to the cause of his country."

Brilliant as was the record of King as the champion of the Sanitary Commission in California it was by no means the beginning and end of his philanthropic labors. The forlorn condition of the Chinese—as men without rights of citizenship—stirred his sympathy and he made earnest effort to secure for them such civic rights as belong to industry. The cause of labor, seldom thought in those days to come within the scope of a minister's interest or duty, commanded his eager attention, and he improved every opportunity to declare his reverence for the world's workers in earth, and stone, and iron. In a fine passage in a lecture on "The Earth and the Mechanic Arts," he writes:

"If we were to choose from the whole planet a score of men to represent us on some other globe or in some other system in a great human fair of the universe, it would not be kings, dukes, prime-ministers, the richest men, we should appoint as ambassadors to show what our race is, and what it is doing here, but the great thinkers, artists, and workers, the thinkers in ink, the thinkers in stone and color, the thinkers in force and homely matter, the men who are bringing the globe up towards the Creator's imagination and purpose; and on this mission the leaders of mechanic art would go side by side with Shakespeare and Milton, Angelo and Wren, Newton and Cuvier.

"In England, now, they are preparing statues of Brunel the engineer, and the Stephensons, father and son, to be finished and erected about the same time with those of Macaulay and Havelock. The nation is beginning to bow to the occupations and the genius that have added to her power ten thousand fold,—is beginning to bow to labor, noble, glorious, sacred labor."

Not alone in public pleas for unpopular causes but in private charity King seemed tireless. "He had the rare facility in everything he said and did of communicating himself; the most precious thing he could bestow." We are told that a multitude in distress came to this overburdened man. Ringing his doorbell they found entrance, and always as they came back, the "step was quicker which was slow before, the head was up which was down before, and the lips wreathed in smiles that were sad before."

Thus we can see that it was not solely his eloquent defense of liberty and justice which caused a San Francisco journal, reporting his funeral, to say, "Perhaps more deeply beloved by a vast number of our people than any other who has lived and toiled and died among us." His good deeds made him worthy of this, one of the most beautiful eulogies ever given mortal man, "No heart ever ached because of him until he died." This was Starr King the philanthropist, a friend to all who needed his friendship.

It would almost appear that in telling the story of "Starr King in California" we were altogether forgetting that he did not come to the State to influence its political action, or even to alleviate poverty and distress. He came as a preacher of Liberal Christianity, and to build up the church that had honored him with a call to its pulpit. Long before he left Boston it was written concerning him, "That he loved his calling, and that it was his ambition to pay the debt which every able man is said to owe to his profession, namely to contribute some work of permanent value to its literature." At that early period a discriminating critic bears testimony, "that his piety, pure, deep, tender, serene and warm, took hold of positive principles of light and beneficence, not the negative ones of darkness and depravity, and—himself a child of light—he preached the religion of spiritual joy."

It was King's first and chief ambition to be an effective preacher. In a letter, written in 1855, he says, "How we do need good preaching. Would that I could preach extempore." A wish that six years later "came true" in his San Francisco pulpit. In the inspiring atmosphere of his new field, and under the stress of a great era, King cast his manuscript aside, and though he made careful preparation, as every man must who speaks worthily, he never again submitted to the bondage of the "written sermon." To a man of King's gifts and temperament this was an immense gain. Indeed, Bostonian Californians were a unit in declaring that Easterners could have no conception of the man and orator Starr King became in those last great years of his brief life.

Speedily the little church in which he preached proved too small for the throng of eager listeners who gathered to hear him, and on the 3d day of December, 1862, the corner stone of a larger and more beautiful edifice was laid.

We shall find it no easy matter to analyze the sources of his power and popularity. Often-times success and failure are equal mysteries. Doubtless no small part of his triumph arose from the peculiar character of the new society to which he brought talents that commanded instant attention. The eager temper of the time fitted his sincere and earnest spirit. It was a perfect adjustment of the man and the hour, the workman and his task.

No small part of his popularity arose from the fact that he insisted upon his right and duty as a minister to discuss great questions of state in the pulpit. The vicious gulf churchmen discover between the sacred and the secular was hidden from his eyes. All that affected the humblest of his fellow men appealed to him as part and parcel of the 'gospel of righteousness he was commissioned to preach. In the old Boston days he had discussed freely in the pulpit such themes as the "Free Soil Movement," "The Fugitive Slave Law," and "The Dred Scott Decision." Burning questions these, and they were handled with no fear of man to daunt the severity of his condemnation when he declared that in the Dred Scott Decision the majority of the Supreme Court had betrayed justice for a political purpose. It was not likely that such a man would remain silent in the pulpit upon the so-called "war issues" of 1861. Early in that memorable year he boldly informed his people as to the course he intended to pursue so long as the war lasted. He would not equivocate and he would not be silent. Henceforth stirring patriotic sermons, as the demand for them arose, were the order of the day in the congregation to which he ministered. The character of these discourses may be partly determined from such titles as, "The Choice between Barabbas and Jesus," "The Treason of Judas Iscariot," "Secession in Palestine," and "Rebellion Pictures from Paradise Lost." "After the lapse of more than sixty years," so the Hon. Horace Davis assured the writer, "I can distinctly remember the fire and passion of those terrible indictments of treason and rebellion."

"Terrible indictments" truly, and in the storm and tempest of the time irresistibly attractive to men and women whose sympathies were on fire for the Northern cause. King's patriotism won for him a liberal hearing on subjects that otherwise the people would have declined to consider.

But we must not forget that "our preacher" was endowed with that rare and radiant gift, an altogether charming and persuasive personality. Appearance, manner, voice, were all instruments of attractiveness, fitting modes of expression to a gentle and noble spirit. When a friend and comrade of King's earlier ministry was asked to name the preacher's preeminent gift, he immediately answered, "his voice." The reply seems trivial. Yet it was seriously spoken by one whose knowledge of King during his Boston ministry was close and personal. William Everett, who had listened to New England's renowned orators, to Emerson's sweet and satisfying voice, and to the music of Wendell Phillip's speech, said of King, "His was one of the noblest and sweetest voices I ever heard." Edward Everett Hale once wrote, "Starr King was an orator, whom no one could silence and no one could answer." Says another, "There was argument in his very voice. It thrilled and throbbed through an audience like an organ carrying conviction captive before its wonderful melody." If it is true that William Pitt once ruled the British Nation by his voice, as good authority affirms, if it is true, that Daniel O'Connell's voice

> *Glided easy as a bird may glide,*
> *And played with each wild passion as it went,*

may it not also be true that Starr King's clear, penetrating, musical voice, answering to the moods of the soul as a loved instrument to the hand of the player, was in itself a kind of gospel of good will to men?

Horace Davis, Starr King's son-in-law, was accustomed to insist that writers had wholly failed to note one element of the great orator's power, namely, his humor. Not wit, Mr. Davis would remark, but a most genial and kindly, and at the same time illuminating humor. A careful examination of King's published sermons, speeches and lectures gives but slight evidence of this gift, owing doubtless to false ideas of what constitutes decorum in the work of a preacher. Occasionally satisfying evidence is found of the truth of Mr. Davis' judgment, as in the following:

"On many a tombstone where it is written, 'Here lies so and so, aged seventy years', the true inscription would read 'In memory of one who in seventy years lived about five minutes and that was when he first fell in love.'"

Writing of his lecture work in California which he called "detestable vagrancy," he says:

"There is a great flood in the interior. California is a lake. Rats, squirrels, locusts, lecturers, and other like pests are drowned out. I am a home bird, and enjoy it hugely."

King greeted the mention of his name as candidate for United States Senator with the statement, "I would swim to Australia before taking a political post," and added, "a dandy lives from one necktie to another, a fashionable woman from one wrinkle to another and a politician from one election to another."

Certainly there is a smile, as well as a truth, in the following:

"Our popular definition of a ghost is just the reverse of truth; it makes one consist of a soul without a body, while really a specter, an illusion, a humbug of the eyesight and the touch, is a human body not vitalized through and through with a soul."

"King was the best story teller of his time," thought Dr. Bellows. "Gifted with an exquisite, a delicious sense of the ludicrous, and given to bursts of uncontrollable merriment, happy as childhood and as innocent," this is the verdict of one of his earliest biographers,—E. P. Whipple. That sunny mirth and infectious laughter was no mean element of his power over the people, we can readily believe.

Another explanation of his far reaching influence both in the pulpit and on the platform, is found in the rare skill with which he made the discoveries of science, and the beauties of nature, serve his need as a teacher of morals and religion. And here, again, he was helped by the spirit of his age. Darwin's "Origin of Species" was published in 1859, a kind of crown and culmination of a half century of brilliant progress in science. Starr King but shared the temper of his time as he turned with delight to the writings of the masters and reveled in the new universe there revealed. Modern science, which troubled the faith of many, only deepened and strengthened his own, as he idealized and spiritualized each new wonder of earth and heaven. The comet of July, 1861, gave noble opportunity to enforce in his pulpit the religious lessons of that mother of all the sciences, Astronomy. "I am glad," he began, "at every new temptation to consider in the pulpit and the Church the wonders and laws of modern astronomy."

"Does it ever occur to you, brethren, how we waste truth? Have you ever felt what a sad thing it is that so little of the vast accumulation of inspiring knowledge should reach our deepest, our religious sentiments, to kindle and feed them? The most certain knowledge which men now hold is that which is gathered from the sky. Astronomy, dealing with objects thousands of millions of miles away, and with forces that rule through limitless space, is the most symmetrical and firm of all the structures of science which have been reared by the human mind. Immeasurably more than David could have known, the heavens, as Herschel reads them, declare the glory of God. Yet how seldom do we think of the splendors and harmonies which a modern book of astronomy unveils as part of God's appeal to our wonder; how seldom does the solemn light from the uppermost regions of immensity, the light of nebulae which science has broken up into heaps of suns, converge upon a human soul with power enough to stimulate devout awe and make the heart bend before the Creator of the universe."

A few days at Lake Tahoe, when not a hundred white men had visited its shores, inspired a sermon long remembered by those who heard it, and today, after numerous nature-sermons by the world's most gifted preachers, this discourse remains an almost perfect example of what such a sermon should be. The following single excerpt must suffice to suggest its beauty:

"I must speak of another lesson, connected with religion, that was suggested to me on the borders of Lake Tahoe. It is bordered by groves of noble pines. Two of the days which I was permitted to enjoy there were Sundays. On one of them I passed several hours of the afternoon in listening, alone, to the murmur of the pines, while the waves were gently beating the shore with their restlessness. If the beauty and purity of the lake were in harmony with the deepest religion of the Bible, certainly the voice of the pines was also in chord with it.

"The oracles of Greece are connected with the oak. And the lightness, the gaiety, the wit, the suppleness, of the Greek mind find in the voice of the oak their fit representatives; for the oak, though so stubborn and sinewy in its substances, is cheery and gay in its tone when the wind strikes it. But the evergreen trees, though so much softer in their stock, are far deeper and more serious in their music; and the evergreen is the Hebrew tree. The Cedar of Lebanon is the tree most prominent when we think of Palestine and the clothing of its hills. As I lay and listened to the deep, serious, yet soft and welcome sound of those pines by the lake shore, I thought of the inspiration of old which had wakened such lasting and wonderful music from the great souls of Israel. When we want knowledge or the quickening of intellect, we enter the groves of Greece; when we would find quickening, when we would feel the deeps of the soul appealed to, we enter the deeper and more sombre woods of Palestine. The voice of the pine helps us to interpret the Hebrew genius. Its range of expression is not so great as that of the oak or the elm or the willow or the beech, but how much richer it is and more welcome in its monotony! How much more profoundly our souls echo it! How much more deeply does it seem to be in harmony with the spirit of the air! What grandeur, what tenderness, what pathos, what heart-searchingness in the swells and cadences of its 'Andante Maestoso,' when the wind wrestles with it and brings out all its soul."

To the graces and gifts we have mentioned it is but necessary to add that King's gospel of religion was in itself a veritable glad tidings to the people. Not a mere deliverance of doubt, or morality veneered with icy culture, but faith clear, strong and radiantly beautiful. His thought of God, of Man, of Immortality, was full of comfort and inspiration. "God is the infinite Christ," he was wont to say. "Jesus revealed under human limitations the mercy and love of the Father."

King rivalled Theodore Parker in the strength and tenderness of his faith that "man is the child of God." Saint and sinner, master and slave, learned and ignorant, rich and poor, all are children of the Infinite God,—

born of His love ere the world was, certain of His love when the world shall have passed away. He felt that if this is not true, there is not enough left of religion to so much as interest an earnest soul. Religion is everything, — the sun in the heavens, — or it is a star too distant, faint and cold, to cast upon our path a single ray of light.

And the unseen world! How very real it was to this man of faith and prayer. The immortal life is the life. These earthly years but lead us thither. Such was his faith. In excess of world-wisdom we say, "Eternity is here and now." Well and good. But if we lose for a kind of technicality the dear old trust in a higher and nobler life beyond the swift-coming night of death, what have we gained? Said our beloved preacher, our "Saint of the Pacific Coast," as he lay dying, "I see a great future before me." Without that vision he would not have been Starr King.

Part V
In Retrospect

Above that of all other men the fame of the orator is transient. Eloquence may be "logic on fire" as Dr. Lyman Beecher defined it. Oratory may be, as Emerson said, "the noblest expression of purely personal energy." But it is so far personal, so allied to grace of gesture, to charm of manner, to melody of voice, to perfection of speech, to a commanding presence, that it carries to the future but a fraction of its power. The cold type and the insentiate page constitute at best only the record of nature's rarest gift.

Moreover oratory today is at its ebb, as it has been a hundred times before, and with us the man of eloquence passes to quick oblivion. It would be futile to deny that the common fate of orators has overtaken Starr King. Even in California the present generation knows painfully little of his great services to the State. This is the first serious attempt, let us hope it will not be the last, accurately to measure the extent and value of that service so nobly rendered. It is gratifying, however, to recall that Californians of his own time, and the years immediately following, paid ample tribute to his work and his memory. Extraordinary honors, such as never have been given to any private citizen, were freely and lovingly accorded the patriot-preacher.

On the evening of March 4, 1864, the day of King's death, the San Francisco Bulletin, then, as now, one of the leading papers of the city, contained the following tribute:

"The announcement of the death of Rev. Thomas Starr King startles the community, and shocks it like the loss of a great battle or tidings of a sudden and undreamed of public calamity. Certainly no other man on the Pacific Coast would be missed so much. San Francisco has lost one of her chief attractions; the State, its noblest orator; the country one of her ablest defenders."

Scarcely forty years of age, a Californian only from 1860 to 1864, he had in this brief period so won the hearts of men that in honor of his funeral the legislature and all the courts adjourned, the national authorities fired minute guns in the bay, while all the flags in the city and on the ships hung at half-mast, including those of the foreign consuls and those on the vessels of England, Russia, Hamburg, Columbia and France. It is believed that in American history no private individual has been so honored by the federal army and by foreign nations.

That Starr King's tomb might serve as a daily reminder to the people of his unique devotion to Union and Liberty, a city ordinance forbidding burials within certain districts of the city was set aside, and to this day his grave can be seen close to one of San Francisco's busy thoroughfares. Nor is this all. One of the giant trees of the Mariposa bears his name and a proud dome of the Yosemite is called Starr King. On the 27th of October, 1892, a beautiful and impressive monument was dedicated in Golden Gate Park to his memory. Its base bears the inscription:

"In him eloquence, strength and virtue were devoted with fearless courage to truth, country and his fellow-men."

The dedication address was given by the Hon. Irving M. Scott, a leading business man of San Francisco. Speaking with the care and sobriety the occasion demanded, Mr. Scott made the following statement, which the writer believes will also be the sober verdict of history:

"We do not say that Starr King determined for California the course which she pursued; but we do say that he was the most potent factor in effecting that determination."

"The most potent factor in effecting that determination," to establish this beyond the possibility of cavil or denial, we have told here once again his inspiring story. The fact that as late as 1913, the Legislature of California appropriated $10,000 to place a bust of Starr King in our National Capitol at Washington would seem to indicate that the people have resolved that this man shall go down to latest generations as par excellence,—"our hero."

It would be natural, and entirely proper, to close by recounting the numerous tributes that in the years since King's death have been paid to his memory, in magazines, memoirs, speeches and poems, but it would seem like sweetness too long drawn out. And, perhaps, few could resist the feeling that no human being ever really deserved such "largeness of love." But they seem so real, they ring so true, that the conviction grows almost to a certainty that here was one who drew men to him by the incarnate sweetness and nobility of his nature. "Doubtless," writes his friend, and co-worker in the Sanitary Commission, Dr. Henry W. Bellows, "he had his own consciousness of imperfection and sin—for he was human, but I have yet to know and yet to hear the first suggestion of what his faults and errors were."

In no spirit of fulsome adulation did a prominent San Franciscan write, on the Sunday following King's departure to "what lies beyond," these tender words, "Bells sadly ringing this Sabbath morning remind me that one pulpit stands empty; and that it must stand empty, to all intents and purposes, until the church walls crumble, and pulpit, pillars, and all are resolved into dust."

Another prominent resident of the State, writing a half century later,— seeing all after the sobering lapse of years, writing as though the cloud of sorrow for his friend had never been lifted, thus pays his sincere tribute of respect:

"And so, in the prime of life, at the zenith of his achievement, before its noon, this sweet, great soul passed away, leaving to those who loved him, dust and anguish. Well do we remember that almost at his death a minor earthquake shook the city, and men said, 'Even the earth shudders at the thought that Starr King is dead.'"

Of the many poetical tributes, two at least, are of permanent significance. One by his friend Bret Harte, dear companion of those great years in San Francisco, on "A Pen of Thomas Starr King," is at once so penetrating and so just that it well deserves here a place:

> *"This is the reed the dead musician dropped,*
> *With tuneful magic in its sheath still hidden;*
> *The prompt allegro of its music stopped,*
> *Its melodies unbidden.*
>
> *But who shall finish the unfinished strain,*
> *Or wake the instrument to awe and wonder,*
> *And bid the slender barrel breathe again,*
> *An organ-pipe of thunder!*
>
> *His pen! what humbler memories cling about*
> *Its golden curves! what shapes and laughing graces*
> *Slipped from its point, when his full heart went out*
> *In smiles and courtly phrases.*
>
> *The truth, half jesting, half in earnest flung;*
> *The word of cheer, with recognition in it;*
> *The note of alms, whose golden speech outrung*
> *The golden gift within it.*
>
> *But all in vain the enchanter's wand we wave:*

No stroke of ours recalls his magic vision:
The incantation that its power gave
Sleeps with the dead magician."

Could Starr King have been given the privilege of selecting his poet-laureate we may be sure he would have named Whittier. For they were both lovers of nature and of man. Both earnest abolitionists, intensely patriotic, loving liberty and the rights of the humblest of God's creatures, they were kindred spirits. So Whittier wrote not alone for New England, not alone for East and West, but from the deeps of his own loyal and gentle soul, as he penned, these beautiful lines:

"The great work laid upon his two-score years
It's done, and well done. If we drop our tears,
Who loved him as few men were ever loved,
We mourn no blighted hope nor broken plan
With him whose life stands rounded and approved
In the full growth and stature of a man.
Mingle, O bells, along the Western slope,
With your deep toll a sound of faith and hope!
Wave cheerily still, O banner, halfway down,
From thousand-masted bay and steepled town!
Let the strong organ with its loftiest swell
Lift the proud sorrow of the land, and tell
That the brave sower saw his ripened grain.
O East and West! O morn and sunset twain
No more forever! —has he lived in vain
Who, priest of Freedom, made ye one and told
Your bridal service from his lips of gold."

Whittier refuses to believe that King's life, though he lived but "two score years" was a "broken plan." All who believe that life is of divine ordering, our days, our duty, our destiny to the last hour will, with resignation, accept this teaching of faith. To others it will seem in the nature of an irreparable loss that one so good, and so greatly useful, should have died so young.

And though he met death with a smile, and said, "Tell my friends that I went lovingly, trustfully, peacefully," yet it is true that he was cut off in the midst of noble dreams of service he would still render humanity. Some one has said that "aspiration, not achievement, is the measure of human worth." If this be true, or partly true, we may not pass in silence the unfulfilled ambitions of Starr King.

His first great dream looked toward a career in Boston. He would found a lectureship, somewhat like, yet most unlike, that afterward conducted by Joseph Cook. How grandly he would have interpreted from such a platform the spiritual significance of modern science is made evident in those great lectures, "Substance and Show," "Laws of Disorder," and in those memorable sermons dealing with natural phenomena. All the progress of more than half a century has not rendered them obsolete. They can still be read with pleasure and profit.

King also planned, when leisure should be afforded him, a work in philosophy. Something of permanent value to all thinkers and students. One needs but to read King's lecture on "Socrates" to understand how rich and valuable such a work would have been. Indeed, here are paragraphs that could have been written only by one of philosophic mood and habit of mind. How much of modern "New Thought Philosophy" is expressed in the following:

"Few acknowledge that thoughts are as substantial as things, that a feeling is as real as a paving stone, that the soul is a congeries of actual forces as truly as the body is, that a moral principle is as persistent and fatal a thing as a chemical agent, and that, in the deeps of the mind and of society, laws are at work as constant and stern as those which spin the planets and heave the sea and poise the firmaments."

Accepting as the ground work of his philosophy such principles as these King tells us that "Socrates came to the conclusion that the stone which his chisel chipped was less substantial than the soul in every human form: and that the beauty which his cunning carved into the block was less charming and permanent than the beauty of truth, temperance, and holiness, which faith and culture could leave upon the invisible essence of man. He therefore resolved to abandon the lower for the higher art of Sculpture, and instead of being an artist in marble to be a fashioner of men."

King's aptness for historical and philosophical generalization is quite evident as we read:

"Socrates was the father of a new method of study. His thoughts were the seed corn of systems. His pupils were the teachers of centuries. Each bump of his brain was the nucleus of a philosophical school. Hardly had he left the world, than the strong and simple light he shed was scattered in various hues by the prismatic minds that had surrounded him or that succeeded him; and in almost every case,—as so often happens when the strands of the solar beam are brilliantly dishevelled,—the actinic ray was lost."

In all our reading we have never met a description of the Grecian philosopher so complete and accurate as one brief phrase in the lecture from which these excerpts are taken, "Socrates, the slouchy ambassador of reason." Or what could be truer of Socrates and Plato than to say that "Arm in arm, the stately duke and the democrat of philosophy walk down the lists of fame?"

Read and re-read the closing paragraph of King's "Socrates" impresses the thoughtful mind more and more by its depth and beauty, and we ask,— what might not this man in his full maturity and in scholarly leisure have contributed to enrich the philosophy of our time?

"Down the River of Life, by its Athenian banks, he had floated upon his raft of reason serene, in cloudy as in smiling weather, for seventy years. And now the night is rushing down, and he has reached the mouth of the stream, and the great ocean is before him, dim heaving in the dusk. But he betrays no fear. There is land ahead, he thought; eternal continents there are, that rise in constant light beyond the gloom. He trusted still in the raft his soul had built, and with a brave farewell to the few true friends who stood by him on the shore he put out into the darkness, a moral Columbus, trusting in his haven on the faith of an idea."

It was an open secret among King's friends in California that he meditated writing of the Yosemite as he had written of the White Hills of New Hampshire. Had he done so that region of incomparable beauty would have been known to the people of our country at least twenty years earlier. What a volume it would have been, "The Beauty and Glory of the Yosemite" by Starr King! What a vision he would have given us of that mighty gorge; of the crystal clearness of Mirror Lake; of the majesty of Cathedral Rock, of Sentinel Dome, or El Capitan; of the bright waterfalls, Vernal and the Bridal Veil; or in exquisite artistry of word painting how he would have pictured for us the wonderful coloring of the Yosemite, the morning tints of gray, the perfect white of noon shading into blue, the afternoon tinge of silver and gold, the sunset's gauze of crimson, and then the varying shades of approaching night. But our artist never lived to paint the picture for us, and are we not the poorer? Is there any such thing in this sad world as superfluous genius? Let our philosophers answer. At all events these were the noble and the unfulfilled ambitions of Starr King.

It would seem that of American statesmen Mr. King most admired Daniel Webster. He never shared the feeling of his fellow abolitionists that Webster's well-known longing to be President had caused him to be false to liberty, but rather that the great "Defender of the Constitution" endeavored to preserve the Union for the sake of liberty. As we have already noted, when the Civil War broke out King found in the service Webster had rendered the Nation some of his strongest arguments for the Northern Cause. He was quite ready to accept the judgment of the English publicist that "Webster was not only the greatest man of his age,—he was the greatest man of any age." No doubt he had followed every stage of that momentous career to the very end. All thoughtful Americans went into retirement with Daniel Webster, and in his last sickness watched in a kind of reverent awe as his life ebbed away. From the solemn death chamber in Marshfield, his home by the stormy Atlantic, came tidings of the great statesman's last moments, in which he repeated, again and again, the Lord's Prayer and the Twenty-third Psalm. Loving friends bore tearful witness to the pathos and heavenly beauty of the old words as they fell from the trembling lips of the dying man, "Yea, though I walk through the valley of the shadow of death, I will fear no evil; for Thou art with me; Thy rod and Thy staff they comfort me."

If it be a coincidence, it is one of striking appropriateness that when the last hour came to our foremost "Defender of the Constitution and the Union," that with unclouded mind, here by the Pacific Sea, he, too, should have passed to his rest, even as the older patriot, whispering with untroubled faith, "The Lord is my shepherd; I shall not want. Yea, though I walk through the valley of the shadow of death, I will fear no evil." "I will fear no evil," these were his last words, and it is good to read that having so spoken, without a struggle or a pang, he entered upon his exceeding great reward. His work on earth was done, and well done.

Here ends Starr King in California, as written by Reverend William Day Simonds, Published in book form by Paul Elder and Company, and seen through their Tomoye Press by Ricardo J. Orozco in the city of San Francisco, during the month of April, Nineteen Hundred and Seventeen.